Anonymous

A brief summary of hypodermic medication:

Compiled for the convenience of the medical practitioner, and issued by

Sharp & Dohme

Anonymous

A brief summary of hypodermic medication:
*Compiled for the convenience of the medical practitioner, and issued by Sharp &
Dohme*

ISBN/EAN: 9783337818241

Printed in Europe, USA, Canada, Australia, Japan

Cover: Foto ©ninafisch / pixelio.de

More available books at **www.hansebooks.com**

A BRIEF SUMMARY

OF

HYPODERMIC MEDICATION.

A

BRIEF SUMMARY

OF

HYPODERMIC MEDICATION,

COMPILED FOR THE CONVENIENCE

OF THE

MEDICAL PRACTITIONER,

AND ISSUED BY

SHARP & DOHME,

BALTIMORE.

1887.

The recent introduction of **soluble hypodermic tablets,** enabling the physician to make an instant solution of a medicinal agent for injection, instead of the bulky solutions, which can be kept unchanged but for a few days, and the improvements in syringes (see plates and description on page 19), have obviated many of the objections to hypodermic medication, and have rendered its practice more sure and easy.

With the view of bringing these facts to the notice of the medical profession, and for their convenient reference in emergencies, we have carefully compiled the following "brief summary" from the most recent and reliable sources.

This summary is necessarily succinct, and should be regarded more in the light of a suggestion and reminder than as an elaborate treatise. We have not only mentioned the remedies which can be furnished in tablet form, but also those liquids which have been used hypodermically.

We hope it will be found convenient for the pocket and prove of substantial service to the busy practitioner, which will be sufficient apology for its publication.

SHARP & DOHME.

BALTIMORE, *April*, 1887.

A BRIEF SUMMARY OF HYPODERMIC MEDICATION, AND ITS ADVANTAGES.

Hypodermic medication has been used now for about twenty-five years—a period sufficient to thoroughly test its value and uses, and to bring the performance of it to a high state of efficiency and accuracy. The following very brief and condensed account is offered in the hope that it will be found of use to the busy practitioner, and may prove suggestive in some emergency when time does not allow the consultation of some more elaborate treatise. To those who desire more fully to enter into this subject, the full and comprehensive work of Prof. Roberts Bartholow, 4th edit. 1882, will give information up to that date.

The advantages of administering remedies by this method are: 1st. A more prompt and speedy effect is produced; indeed, the effects of active remedies thrown into the connective tissue under the skin are perceived almost instantaneously. 2d. The results are more permanent and curative. In the case of neuralgia, for example, remedies are often given without effect, and for some time, when their hypodermic use has promptly wrought a cure. A very simple explanation of this is found in the fact that many remedies themselves undergo changes when brought in contact with the gastric juice, and even if not altered, their absorption is necessarily slow; consequently they do not make that forcible impression which is made when they are given hypodermically. 3d. Gastric disturbances are avoided. Remedies do not interfere with a digestion often already enfeebled. 4th, and finally, remedies can be administered to persons unable or unwilling to swallow—as in the case of unconsciousness from narcotic poisons, persons with suicidal intent, or the mentally deranged.

Various objections have been made to this method; but when these are examined they will be found to depend on imperfect instruments, badly prepared medicinal agents, or an improper introduction of the medicinal agent. 1st. The instrument should be kept clean and in good working order; the needle-points sharp and free from rust. 2d. The solution for injection should be *freshly* prepared, and of medicinal agents of undoubted purity and strength. 3d. The injection must be made *under the skin* into the connective tissue. A failure to observe one or all of these conditions may involve the formation of abscesses, or even serious systemic effects. Dangerous results have followed the injection of some powerful remedy into a vein. but a little care on the part of the operator will avoid any such accident.

The instrument itself has been made of various materials and modified in many ways since its first use. There is no one substance presenting all the qualities needed to form an ideally perfect hypodermic syringe; the one combining most of these qualities is glass, and its single disadvantage of fragility has been successfully overcome by enclosing the glass barrel in a bi-fenestrated cylinder of metal. An instrument thus made has the advantage of not being acted upon by any agents likely to be used subcutaneously; of being transparent to allow of the inspection of its contents, and of being easily kept clean. The needles should be of finely tempered steel, with needle-point and sharp cutting edges, so as readily to pierce the integument without any bruising. Care should be taken that they are kept free from rust and that the entire syringe is regularly cleansed after use and before being placed in its case. This can be done by drawing in and forcing out several times a little clean water; unscrewing the needle and carefully wiping the point dry between the fingers; the small quantity of sebaceous matter from the skin being sufficient to prevent it from rusting. A fine wire should then be inserted to keep the tube of the needle open. Very great improvements have lately been added in furnishing what are called wings to the syringe, giving a firm hold and complete control of the instrument; and in making the lower cap movable, exposing the whole calibre of the barrel and allowing the introduction of a tablet, thus *making a solution in the syringe.*

The operation of injection is a very simple one. The place chosen for its performance is usually the outer side of the arm, but any convenient place will answer. Some authorities prefer injecting at or near the seat of pain. Inflamed tissues and bony prominences should be avoided. The place being determined, a fold of loose skin is pinched up between the thumb and finger of the left hand. The syringe being charged. the needle is thrust in promptly, penetrating the skin. This will be recognized by the cessation of resistance, and the point of the needle will now move freely in the connective tissue. The needle should pass in an inch or more. The piston is now slowly pushed home; the needle is then withdrawn and pressure with the point of a finger should be made for a few moments, to prevent the escape of the fluid. In cases of paralysis, some inject directly into a muscle. Prof. Bartholow, "Hypodermatic Medication," p. 44, says : "In practising the hypodermatic injection, it is important to avoid puncturing a vein. Serious depression of the powers of life, fainting, and sudden and profound narcotism, have been produced by injecting a solution of morphia directly into a vein. Fatal collapse might be induced by injecting air into a large vein along with the solution." This latter may be avoided by driving all the air out of the syringe, after charging it, by holding the syringe with the needle-point up and gently pushing the piston until a drop of fluid exudes.

The active agent to be injected subcutaneously should be in perfect solution. The solution itself should be neutral (*i. e.* neither acid nor alkaline), clear and free from foreign matter, and not too concentrated. The difficulty of fulfilling these conditions has in the past very materially hindered the more general use of this method of treatment. But comparatively a very few years ago many of the alkaloids were to be had only as bases, and were more or less insoluble without the addition of some acid, and the slightest excess of the latter caused intense local irritation. When this had been overcome, after a clear, neutral solution had been made, it was found impossible to preserve it in this state for even a short time. It was found that even after a few days a solution of morphine which had been carefully filtered and was perfectly clear had become cloudy. This was owing to the growth of a microscopic organism, the *Penicilium;* and experience proved that this not only grew at the expense of the alkaloid, thus weakening the strength of the solution, but that it proved also to be a local irritant when injected into the tissues, resulting frequently in abscess. From time to time various means were devised to obviate this difficulty, but none proved effectual until the soluble hypodermic tablets were made. These, when properly prepared, solve the problem most satisfactorily. They should be quickly and entirely soluble, perfectly neutral, and the excipient combined with the alkaloid should be bland and unirritating. Made in this manner they are a great boon to the profession, since they reduce the dose to a mathematical accuracy, which was formerly very often a matter of conjecture, when a solution had to be carried about. The alkaloid is effectually preserved in the tablet from deterioration, and the latter presents an accurate and definite dose, of which a solution can be made fresh, and almost instantaneously, when needed. Their portability and compactness are not the least among their good qualities. The practitioner can now go armed with a dozen hypodermic remedies, which will not deterioriate by keeping, and which do not occupy any more space than formerly the vial containing a solution of morphine alone did.

Prof. Bartholow, p. 59, says: "A 'hypodermic tablet' .... is conveniently carried, and, as regards liability to accident, is much superior to any permanent solution. Since I have adopted the method of extemporaneous solutions, I have not had occur the hard nodules and the points of suppuration and sloughing which were not infrequent when permanent solutions were employed."

Remedies used hypodermically are much more active than when given by the mouth.

The general rule is to give **one-third less** than given by the mouth to produce the same impression. As some persons exhibit peculiar susceptibilities to certain remedies, it would be well to inject a small dose tentatively where the idiosyncrasy of the patient is not known.

Apomorphine used hypodermically is indispensable as an emetic in cases of narcotic poisoning. It acts freely when all emetics given by the mouth fail. It has also been used in *capillary bronchitis* to free the tubes of secretion, and in *croup* to dislodge the false membrane.

Amyl nitrite is usually best given by inhalation, but where respiration is about ceasing, as in cases of *angina pectoris, chloroform narcosis, surgical shock, cholera asphyxia,* etc., etc., it may prove of immense utility when injected hypodermically.

Arsenic has been successfully used in *chorea, lymphadenoma, enlarged spleen* and in *splenic leucocythemia*. Excellent results have also been obtained in chronic skin diseases, as *psoriasis* and *eczema*. The best form is **sodium arseniate,** which is less likely to produce the toxic effects of arsenic than any other, and is less irritant locally.

Atropine is principally used in combination with morphine, and as its physiological antagonist. It has been used to advantage by hypodermic injection in *acute rheumatism* near the painful joint, in *epilepsy*, and *asthma* with marked results. *Seasickness* and *vomiting of pregnancy* are relieved by it ; the algid state of *cholera ; diseases of the bladder.* Atropine is also the antagonist to pilocarpine, muscarine and eserine, and may be used to combat the toxic effects of these, as well as of morphine or opium. In treating a case of poisoning by atropine, it should be remembered that its effects on the economy last longer than those of morphine, so that, in giving the latter as an antidote, it may be necessary to repeat the dose of morphine.

Caffeine has been used in *neuralgia, hysterical headache* and *migraine.* Dr. Anstie relieved by it the *insomnia* attendant upon chronic alcoholism without delirium. It has also been used with success against *opium narcosis.*

Carbolic acid used hypodermically as a 2 per cent. solution, has produced excellent results in *erysipelas*, and in *other diseases* supposed to depend on morbific ferments. It has also been used in *pleuro-pneumonia*, in *synovitis, white swelling, adenoma, bubo, fibroma*, etc. It has afforded great relief in *acute rheumatism*, in *chronic rheumatism, myalgia, superficial neuralgia*, etc.

Chloral hydrate causes much local irritation and pain when injected under the skin—so much so that its use is restricted to cases in which the stomach cannot bear the remedy, or where the patient is unable or unwilling to swallow. It has proved useful in *poisoning by strychnine, uncontrollable vomiting, obstinate hiccough*, in *violent cholera morbus*, and in *true cholera*. In the latter Prof. Bartholow had the best results from its use. It has also proved beneficial in *asthma* and other *neuroses of the chest*, but care must be exercised lest a fatal result is produced by paralysis of a weak heart.

Chloroform is not adapted for ordinary hypodermic use, but has been used with great success in many cases of obstinate *neuralgia, sciatica*, etc., by a *deep* injection, by Prof. Bartholow. For details, see his work on "Hypodermatic Medication," fourth edition, 1882, p. 288, etc.

Cocaine is principally used subcutaneously for producing local anæsthesia in minor surgical operations, etc. For this purpose it is injected into the areolar tissue as near to the seat of operation as possible. Also injected into the gum for drawing teeth. Recently Bignon found that animals poisoned by strychnine can be saved by the hypodermic injection of cocaine pushed to the point of delirium, and the effect

10

maintained for some time. He found they could be saved by this means even after the occurrence of tetanic spasms. See *Medical News*, December 25th. 1886.

Codeine may be used hypodermically as a substitute for morphine, but has no advantages except where a special hypnotic action is desired, as in *mania, hypochondria*, and *delirium tremens*. It has proved of great use in *diabetes*.

Conine has been used in *asthma, emphysema, angina pectoris, tetanus*, and in *acute mania*.

Curarine or **Woorarine** has been used in *tetanus* with some success. It has also been used in *epilepsy* and in *hydrophobia* with reported success.

Duboisine may be substituted for atropine in all diseases where the latter is now used. Prof. Bartholow is of opinion that it is to be preferred to atropine, and gives it as his experience that it is much more effective in *psychical disorders*.

Ergotin hypodermically is available for *hemorrhages* in general ; especially useful in *hæmoptysis. subinvolution of the uterus, chronic metritis. intramural fibroids, polypi* and *hydatid mole of uterus, hypertrophied prostate, varicocele, aneurism. varicose veins, enlarged spleen, leukaemia, exophthalmic goitre, acute affections of the meninges of the brain* and *spinal cord, cerebro-spinal meningitis, congestive form of migraine* and *headache. sunstroke, tic douloureux. hemicrania,* and sometimes in *sciatica*.

Eserine or **Physostigmine** has been of great utility in *tetanus*, the proportion of recoveries to deaths being one-half. It should be given hypodermically and in quantities sufficient to keep the spasms in check, and sufficient nourishment must be given. It has also been used in *hydrophobia*, in *bronchitis, pulmonary congestion* and *pneumonia*.

Ether may be employed subcutaneously with great advantage in cases of sudden depression of the powers of life, as in the *bites of venomous snakes, surgical shock, Asiatic cholera,* the passage of biliary or renal calculi ; in the action of arterial sedatives, as aconite, veratrum viride, etc. Also in *cardiac failure* from *hemorrhage*. It has proved of great benefit in cases of severe *adynamic pneumonia,* and in *variola*. It should *never* be used in the *chloroform narcosis*. **Whiskey** or **brandy** may be used hypodermically in cases of sudden depression of the powers of life, but *not* in the *chloroform narcosis*. They are more likely to be conveniently at hand in sudden emergencies than ether, but are more apt to be followed by local inflammation and abscess.

Hydrocyanic acid may be given subcutaneously with advantage in *mental disorders, gastralgia, nausea* and *vomiting*.

Hyoscine is derived from the decomposition of Hoscyamine and is said to possess the sedative and hypnotic properties of Hyoscyamine in a much higher degree, and may be used in its stead.

Hyoscyamine is of high value in *mental disorders, paralysis agitans, chorea, mercurial trembling, senile trembling, spasmodic cough, laryngismus, hiccough.*

Mercury, in the form of **corrosive chloride,** by the hypodermic method is used in *syphilis,* and with the greatest advantage ; also in some forms of chronic skin diseases. Corrosive chloride of mercury generally causes some pain when used subcutaneously, but with a solution not too concentrated, with a clean syringe and sharp-cutting needle without rust, there is no danger of an abscess.

Morphine alone or combined with **Atropine** has proved useful in *diseases of the brain* and *nervous system, delirium tremens, cerebro-spinal meningitis, sunstroke, hysteria, epilepsy, eclampsia, uraemic convulsions, chorea, tetanus, hydrophobia, muscular cramp and spasm, neuralgia.* Also in *asthma, emphysema, hiccough, acute inflammatory affections of the respiratory organs, angina pectoris, dyspepsia, schirrus, cholera, vomiting of pregnancy, colic, peritonitis, affections of the bladder and urethra, after-pains in childbirth, the nocturnal pains in acute rheumatism* and *tertiary syphilis;* in certain *surgical diseases,* especially *fractures* and *dislocations, strangulated hernia;* as an aid to *chloroform narcosis,* and in *poisoning* by belladonna or atropine, by gelsemium, and by veratrum viride.

As **Morphine** is by far the most frequently used subcutaneously of the alkaloids, and its range of usefulness is very large, it is well to bear in mind that a larger dose can be given combined with atropine, since the latter is a powerful excitant of the centre of respiration, which is depressed by large doses of morphine, and a fatal issue may result in consequence of paralysis of this centre. The desirable effects of morphine are increased by the addition of atropine, while the toxic effects are counteracted.

Should toxic symptoms be induced by the use of morphine, they should be met with a subcutaneous injection of atropine. The head of the patient should be low, all restrictions to free respiration removed, ammonia placed to the nostrils. Subsequently caffeine may be given hypodermically. Artificial respiration and the faradic current to the muscles of the chest may be used. The injection of ammonia into the veins, and the inhalation of amyl nitrite or its injection subcutaneously, have proved of benefit.

Nicotine has been successful in *tetanus*. About one half the traumatic cases treated with it recover. The officinal wine of tobacco may be substituted for the alkaloid.

Pilocarpine has been advantageously used in *mumps* and *acute affections of the parotid, submaxillary* and *sublingual glands, acute tonsilitis.* Has afforded relief in the *metastasis* of *mumps, obstinate hiccough, hoarseness, bronchitis, bronchorrhœa, asthma, emphysema, cardiac dropsy, dropsy of acute albuminuria, eclampsia, effusion into cavities.* To cut short an *ague chill.*
It may be administered either as nitrate or muriate.

Quinine has been used subcutaneously with great advantage in *pernicious fever*, in *malarial fevers* attended with *gastric irritation*, in *chronic malarial poisoning*, to abort recent *malarial fevers;* combined with a small dose of morphine it has proved very useful in *typhoid fever*. It has also been used very successfully in India in the treatment of *sunstroke*. Finally, some cases of *neuralgia* have been cured by its means. The form best adapted to hypodermic use is the quinina bi-muriatica carbamidata, which produces no local irritation.

Strychnine injected under the skin has proved highly beneficial in the treatment of *paralysis*, especially in *hemiplegia*, *paraplegia*, *infantile paralysis*, *local paralysis, progressive muscular atrophy, progressive locomotor ataxia, facial paralysis, gastralgia, cardiac neuralgia, amaurosis, amblyopia*. In the misty vision produced by the abusive use of tobacco, strychnine has been found to be of the greatest advantage in restoring strength to the optic nerve.

Dr. Echeverria remarks : " The effects of strychnia are widely different when administered hypodermically or by the mouth. A smaller dose exhibited hypodermically may be capable of regenerating at once the lost muscular power."

SHARP & DOHME'S

SOLUBLE

HYPODERMIC TABLETS.

**Perfectly and quickly soluble.
Always ready for instant use.
Never cause local irritation.**

These tablets are confidently offered to the medical profession as combining every possible merit.

They can be perfectly and quickly dissolved when dropped into a little water in the barrel of our Improved Hypodermic Syringe (see page 19) and shaken.

They are accurate in dose, and retain their activity and strength for any length of time.

They may also be given by the mouth.

SOLUBLE HYPODERMIC TABLETS.		Per Bottle 100 Tab's	Per Bottle 20 Tab's
APOMORPHINE MURIATE	1-20 gr	$ 80	20
" "	1-12 gr	1 00	25
" "	1-8 gr	1 20	35
ATROPINE SULPHATE	1-150 gr	40	15
" "	1-100 gr	40	15
" "	1-60 gr	55	17
CAFFEINE SODIO-BENZOATE	1-2 gr	90	25
" "	1 gr	1 10	30
COCAINE HYDROCHLORATE	1-25 gr	70	20
" "	1-10 gr	90	25
" "	1-8 gr	90	25
" "	1-4 gr	1 50	35
" "	1-2 gr	2 40	60

SOLUBLE HYPODERMIC TABLETS.

		Per Bottle 100 Tab's	Per Bottle 20 Tab's
CODEINE SULPHATE	1-8 gr	$ 70	20
"	1-4 gr	1 00	25
CONINE HYDROBROMATE	1-50 gr	70	20
DUBOISINE SULPHATE	1-100 gr	70	20
"	1-60 gr	1 00	25
ERGOTIN	1 10 gr	70	20
ESERINE SULPHATE	1-100 gr	1 00	25
" "	1-50 gr	1 10	30
HYOSCYAMINE SULPHATE	1-100 gr	1 20	35
HYOSCINE HYDROBROMATE	1 100 gr	2 00	50
MERCURY CORROSIVE CHLORIDE	1-60 gr	40	15
" "	1-40 gr	40	15
MORPHINE SULPHATE	1-8 gr	50	15
" "	1-6 gr	55	17
" "	1-4 gr	60	18
" "	1-3 gr	90	25
" "	1-2 gr	1 10	30
MORPHINE AND ATROPINE No. I. { Morphine.. 1-8 gr } { Atropine...1-200 gr }		60	16
MORPHINE AND ATROPINE No. II. { Morphine...1-6 gr } { Atropine...1-180 gr }		65	18
MORPHINE AND ATROPINE No. III. { Morphine... 1-4 gr } { Atropine .1-150 gr }		70	20
MORPHINE AND ATROPINE No. IV. { Morphine...1-4 gr } { Atropine...1-100 gr }		90	25
PILOCARPINE MURIATE	1-20 gr	90	25
" "	1-8 gr	1 20	35
" "	1-3 gr	3 00	65
PILOCARPINE NITRATE	1-20 gr	90	25
" "	1-8 gr	1 20	35
" "	1-3 gr	3 00	65
QUININE BIMURIATE CARBAM	1 gr	1 10	25
" "	2 gr	2 10	45
" "	3 gr	3 10	65
SODIUM ARSENIATE	1-30 gr	40	15
STRYCHNINE SULPHATE	1-150 gr	40	15
" "	1-120 gr	40	15
" "	1-100 gr	40	15
" "	1-60 gr	40	15

☞ Tablets Can be Sent by Mail If Desired.

LATEST IMPROVED
HYPODERMIC SYRINGE,

MANUFACTURED EXPRESSLY FOR

SHARP & DOHME.

This syringe is represented by Fig. 3. The very important improvements consist of the movable cap *a*, which opens the entire calibre of the barrel and allows the easy introduction of our soluble tablets, and a solution for *immediate* use is readily made by adding 10 m. water. Then the solid and securely fastened wing-plate affords a firm hold and perfect command of the syringe.

They are packed either in an oblong leather-covered case (Fig. 1) 3 inches long, 1⅝ inches wide, containing, besides the syringe, two bottles of our soluble tablets; or in a flat nickel-plated metal case (Fig. 2) 3¼ inches long by 1⅝ inches wide, containing one bottle of tablets besides the syringe. They are all of the best materials and most accurately made.

A SYRINGE

packed in either style of case as described above will
be sent by mail on receipt of
$2.50.

18

Fig. 3.

a

Fig. 1.

Fig. 2.